Eating

A Healthy Cookbook with Healthy Recipes for Clean Eating Everyday

By
BookSumo Press
All rights reserved

Published by
http://www.booksumo.com

ENJOY THE RECIPES?

KEEP ON COOKING WITH 6 MORE FREE COOKBOOKS!

Visit our website and simply enter your email address to join the club and receive your 6 cookbooks.

http://booksumo.com/magnet

https://www.instagram.com/booksumopress/

https://www.facebook.com/booksumo/

LEGAL NOTES

All Rights Reserved. No Part Of This Book May Be Reproduced Or Transmitted In Any Form Or By Any Means. Photocopying, Posting Online, And / Or Digital Copying Is Strictly Prohibited Unless Written Permission Is Granted By The Book's Publishing Company. Limited Use Of The Book's Text Is Permitted For Use In Reviews Written For The Public.

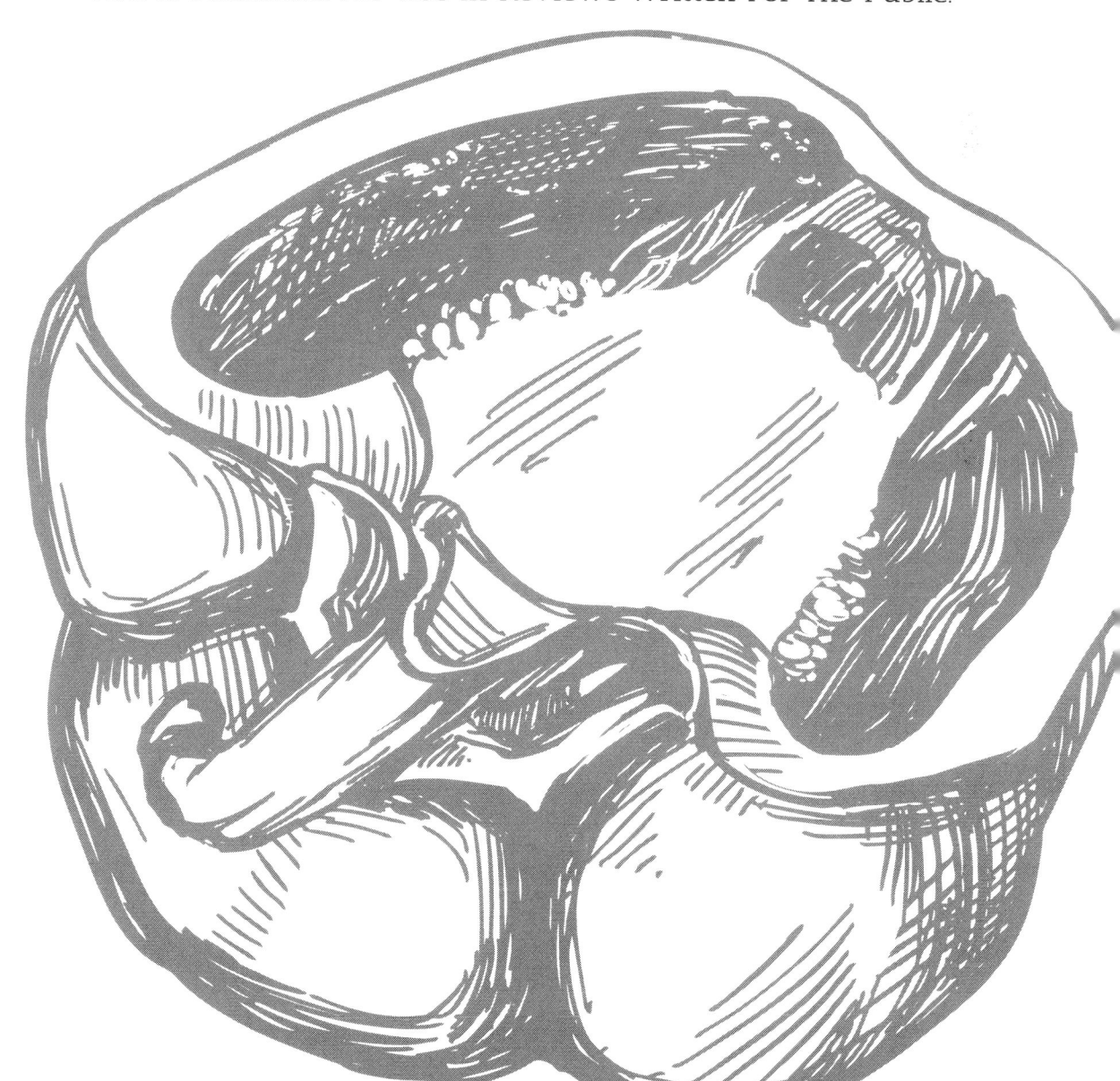

Table of Contents

Blackened Chicken Cutlets 9

Grilled Salad 10

Mendoza Kabobs 11

Grilled Gazebo Salad 12

Endive on the Grill 13

Southwest Sirloin 14

Fruity Pasta Salad 15

Dijon Orange Fruit Salad 16

Basmati Fruit Salad 17

Glazed Radish Fruit Salad 18

Fruit Salad Jakarta 19

Seattle Creamy Quinoa Salad 20

2nd Grade Fruit Salad 21

Caribbean Honeydew and Guava Salad 22

5-Ingredient Chinese Salad 23

Memphis Inspired Fruit Salad 24

Mi Tia's Fruit Salad 25

Sweet Balsamic Dates Salad 26

Blackberry Raspberry Salad 27

Fruit Salad Minnetonka 28

Maui Pineapple Salad 29

Fruit Salad with the Works 30

Simple Ceviche Formulae 31

Full Barcelona Ceviche 32

Ferdinand's Favorite 33

Hot Hawaiian Ceviche 34

Imitation Ceviche 35

Arizona Shrimp Ceviche 36

Southern Sole Ceviche 37

Spiced Kale Ceviche 38

Ceviche Cups 39

Boardwalk Ceviche 40

Wednesday's Lunch Ceviche 41

Louisiana Ceviche 42

Catalina's Cabbage Ceviche 43

West Indian Ceviche 44

Bahamian Ceviche 45

New England Ceviche Bowls 46

Sunday's Ceviche 47

Isabelle's Ceviche 48

Peruvian Salad Dressing 49

Simple Pesto 50

How to Make Hummus 51

Mediterranean Red Hummus 52

Black Bean Hummus 53

Mesa Mediterranean Chicken Wraps 54

Trinidad Rotisserie Wraps 55

Mexicana Wraps 56

Garden Turkey Pesto Wraps 57

Picante Bean Wraps 58

Mediterranean Cheese Wraps 59

Japanese Spring Roll Wraps 60

Dijon Genoa Wraps 61

Pesto Tilapia Lettuce Wraps 62

Bangkok Meets Morocco Wraps 63

Bacon Lettuce and Tomato Wraps 64

Guyanese Chickpea Wraps 65

Cashew Butter Wraps 66

Spicy Turkey Wraps 67

West African Peanut Wraps 68

Mexican Tuna Rolls 69

Moscow Beef Wraps 70

Chipotle Bean Wraps 71

Hot Hawaiian Wraps 72

Napa Valley Wraps 73

California Wraps with Thai Spicy Mayo 74

Hot Breakfast Wraps 75

Ketogenic String Bean Wraps 76

Pennsylvania Cheese Wraps 77

Island Coconut Wraps 78

How to Make Cabbage 79

Jamaican Cabbage 80

Brown Glazed Carrots 81

Jamaican Roast 82

Nutty Jerk Coleslaw 83

Flame Broiled Sweet Potatoes 84

Simple Banana Chips 85

Coconut Cod Stew 86

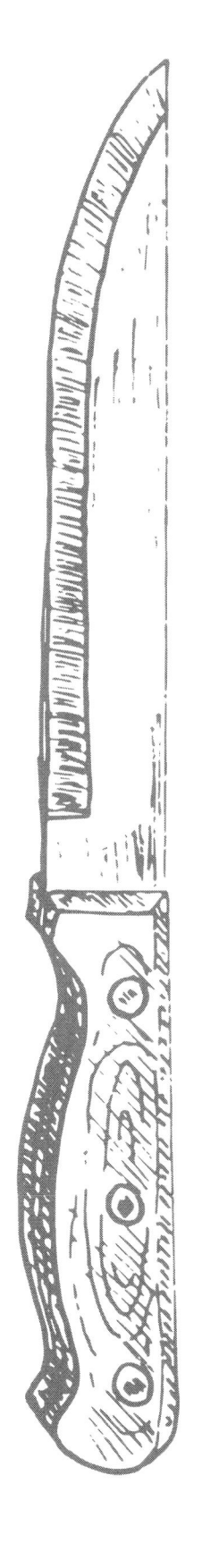

Skirt Steak Habanero Sauce 87

Tropical Prawns Skillet 88

Tropical Vegetarian Papaya Soup 89

Spicy Mango Papaya Salsa 90

Papaya Boats 91

Avocado Papaya Salsa 92

Island Juice 93

Blackened Chicken Cutlets

Prep Time: 5 mins
Total Time: 13 mins

Servings per Recipe: 4
Calories   154.2
Fat   1.7 g
Cholesterol   68.4 mg
Sodium   1836.4 mg
Carbohydrates   5.3 g
Protein   28.2 g

Ingredients

4 -6 boneless skinless chicken breast halves
Spice Mix
4 tsp granulated onion
4 tsp granulated garlic
1 tbsp kosher salt
2 tsp chili powder
2 tsp ground black pepper
extra virgin olive oil

Directions

1. Before you do anything, preheat the grill and grease it.
2. Get a mixing bowl: Combine in it the onion with garlic, salt, chili powder and black pepper.
3. Coat the chicken dices with the spice mixture. Thread them onto skewers.
4. Grill them for 10 to 14 min. Serve them warm.
5. Enjoy.

GRILLED
Salad

Prep Time: 10 mins
Total Time: 16 mins

Servings per Recipe: 4
Calories   126.5
Fat   8.4 g
Cholesterol   2.2 mg
Sodium   72.4 mg
Carbohydrates   11.0 g
Protein   4.9 g

Ingredients

2 tbsp extra virgin olive oil
1 tbsp lemon juice
1 small garlic clove, minced
1/2 tsp Dijon mustard
1/8 tsp Worcestershire sauce
1/4 tsp black pepper

2 tbsp grated parmesan cheese
olive oil flavored cooking spray
2 romaine lettuce hearts

Directions

1. Get a mixing bowl: Mix in it the oil, lemon juice, garlic, mustard, Worcestershire, and pepper.
2. Add the parmesan cheese and combine them well to make the dressing.
3. Place it in the fridge until ready to serve.
4. Before you do anything, preheat the grill and grease it.
5. Slice the romaine hearts in half lengthwise. Coat them with a cooking spray.
6. Grill them for 3 to 4 min on each side. Serve them warm with the cheese dressing.
7. Enjoy.

Mendoza Kabobs

🥣 Prep Time: 30 mins
🕐 Total Time: 45 mins

Servings per Recipe: 4
Calories   532.5
Fat   40.9 g
Cholesterol   92.8 mg
Sodium   96.2 mg
Carbohydrates   9.7 g
Protein   31.5 g

Ingredients

- 4 chicken breasts, diced
- 1/2 red bell pepper, cut into squares
- 1/2 green bell pepper, cut into squares
- 2 yellow onions, cut into eighths
- 1 C. cherry tomatoes
- bamboo skewer
- 1/2 C. oil
- 3 cloves garlic, chopped
- 1 tsp paprika
- 1/2 tsp Mexican oregano
- kosher salt
- black peppercorns

Directions

1. Before you do anything, preheat the grill and grease it.
2. Get a food processor: Combine in it the Oil, Garlic, Paprika, Oregano, Salt, and Peppercorns.
3. Process them several times until they become smooth to make the marinade.
4. Get a large mixing bowl: Combine in it the chicken dices with marinade.
5. Cover the bowl and let it sit for at least 20 min.
6. Before you do anything else, preheat the grill and grease it.
7. Thread the chicken dices with onion, peppers, and cherry tomatoes onto skewers while alternating between them.
8. Grill them for 8 to 10 min on each side. Serve them warm.
9. Enjoy.

GRILLED
Gazebo Salad

Prep Time: 15 mins
Total Time: 25 mins

Servings per Recipe: 8
Calories	336.1
Fat	18.2 g
Cholesterol	29.5 mg
Sodium	428.5 mg
Carbohydrates	32.6 g
Protein	10.7 g

Ingredients

Vegetables
4 cloves roasted garlic, minced
1 red pepper, quartered
1 portabella mushroom
1 onion, sliced
1 zucchini, sliced into 4 long strips
3 tbsp olive oil
3 tbsp balsamic vinegar
tsp Italian seasoning
Dressing
2 cloves garlic, minced

1/4 C. olive oil
1/8 C. balsamic vinegar
1 sprig rosemary, stem discarded leaves chopped
Salad
16 oz. cheese tortellini
1/2 C. provolone cheese, diced
4 oz. black olives
salt and pepper

Directions

1. Get a large zip lock bag: Combine in it the veggies with oil, vinegar, and Italian seasoning.
2. Seal the bag and let them sit for 60 min in the fridge.
3. Before you do anything, preheat the grill and grease it.
4. Grill the veggies for 3 to 4 min on each side.
5. Place them aside to cool down for a bit. Dice them.
6. Get a food processor: Combine in it the salad dressing ingredients. Blend them smooth.
7. Get a large mixing bowl: Combine in it the grilled veggies with tortellini, cheese, olives, dressing, a pinch of salt and pepper.
8. Stir them to coat. Adjust the seasoning of your salad then serve it with extra toppings of your choice.
9. Enjoy.

Endive on the Grill

Prep Time: 10 mins
Total Time: 15 mins

Servings per Recipe: 4
Calories   151.0
Fat   7.7 g
Cholesterol   0.0 mg
Sodium   113.9 mg
Carbohydrates   18.0 g
Protein   6.4 g

Ingredients

olive oil
4 Belgian endive halved lengthwise and trimmed
2 tbsp olive oil
1 tbsp oregano, chopped

1 tbsp balsamic vinegar
salt & ground black pepper

Directions

1. Before you do anything, preheat the grill and grease it.
2. Get a large mixing bowl: Toss in it the endive halves with oil, 1/2 tbsp of oregano, a pinch of salt and pepper.
3. Place them on the grill and let them cook for 4 to 5 min on each side.
4. Transfer the grilled endive halves to a serving plate.
5. Drizzle over them some vinegar. Garnish them with some oregano then serve them warm.
6. Enjoy.

SOUTHWEST Sirloin

Prep Time: 10 mins
Total Time: 20 mins

Servings per Recipe: 4
Calories   180.1
Fat   5.5 g
Cholesterol   68.0 mg
Sodium   453.9 mg
Carbohydrates   6.6 g
Protein   26.1 g

Ingredients

3 tbsp chili powder
2 tsp brown sugar
2 tsp pepper
2 garlic cloves, minced
1/2 tsp salt
1/2 tsp dried oregano

1/4 tsp ground cumin
1 lb. boneless beef top sirloin steak
salsa

Directions

1. Get a mixing bowl: Mix in it the chili powder, brown sugar, pepper, garlic, salt, oregano, and cumin.
2. Massage the mixture into the steak and let it sit for at least 30 min.
3. Before you do anything, preheat the grill and grease it.
4. Grill it for 6 to 8 min on each side. Serve it warm with some salsa.
5. Enjoy.

Fruity Pasta Salad

Prep Time: 30 mins
Total Time: 40 mins

Servings per Recipe: 6
Calories   337.0
Fat   7.1g
Cholesterol   0.8mg
Sodium   43.5mg
Carbohydrates   60.4g
Protein   11.0g

Ingredients

- 8 oz. medium pasta shells
- 1 C. nonfat plain yogurt
- 1 tbsp honey
- 1/4 C. frozen orange juice concentrate, thawed
- 1 (11 oz.) cans mandarin oranges, drained
- 1 C. red seedless grapes, halved
- 1 C. green seedless grapes, halved
- 1 apple, cored and chopped
- 1/2 C. celery, sliced
- 1/2-3/4 C. black walnut

Directions

1. In a pan of the salted boiling water, cook the pasta as directed on the package.
2. Drain the pasta and place into a bowl.
3. Keep aside to cool.
4. In another bowl, add the honey, yogurt and orange juice concentrate and mix until well combined.
5. In the bowl of the pasta, add the remaining ingredients except oranges and yogurt mixture and toss to combine well.
6. Add the oranges and gently, toss to combine.
7. Cover the bowl and refrigerate to chill completely.
8. Enjoy chilled.

DIJON Orange Fruit Salad

Prep Time: 20 mins
Total Time: 40 mins

Servings per Recipe: 6
Calories 171.9
Fat 9.3g
Cholesterol 0.0mg
Sodium 35.8mg
Carbohydrates 23.3g
Protein 1.3g

Ingredients

3 large carrots, peeled and grated
1/4 peeled and cored pineapple, chopped
1 navel orange, peeled and sectioned
1 large tart apple, cored and chopped
1/4 C. raisins

2 Valencia oranges, juice
1/4 C. extra virgin olive oil
1 tsp Dijon mustard
salt & ground black pepper

Directions

1. In a bowl, add the fruit, carrots and raisins and mix.
2. In another bowl, add the mustard, oil, orange juice, salt and pepper to and mix until well combined.
3. Pour the dressing over the salad and gently, toss to coat well.
4. Refrigerate to chill completely.
5. Enjoy chilled.

Basmati Fruit Salad

Prep Time: 45 mins
Total Time: 1 hr 5 mins

Servings per Recipe: 6
Calories	379.1
Fat	7.4g
Cholesterol	0.0mg
Sodium	401.2mg
Carbohydrates	74.5g
Protein	6.3g

Ingredients

- 2 C. uncooked basmati rice, rinsed well and drained
- 1 tbsp peanut oil
- 1/4 C. chopped green onion
- 2 garlic cloves, minced
- 1 tbsp curry powder
- 1 tbsp minced ginger
- 1 tsp salt
- 3 1/2 C. water
- 2 apples, diced
- 1 1/2 C. well drained crushed pineapple
- 1/2 C. diced dried apricot
- 1/4 C. unsweetened flaked coconut
- 1/4 C. chopped mint
- 1/4 C. chopped cilantro
- salt and pepper

Dressing
- 1/2 C. mango chutney, see appendix
- 2 tbsp squeezed lemon juice
- 1 tsp canola oil
- 1 tsp honey

Directions

1. In a pot, add the oil over medium heat and cook until heated through.
2. Add the rice, green onions, ginger, garlic and curry powder and stir fry for about 3-4 minutes.
3. Add the water and 1 tsp of the salt and stir to combine.
4. Set the heat to low and simmer, covered for about 15 minutes.
5. Remove from the heat and with a fork, fluff the rice.
6. Keep aside to cool.
7. In a bowl, add the rice, pineapple, apples, coconut, apricots, cilantro and mint and mix until well blended.
8. For the dressing: in a food processor, add all the ingredients and pulse until smooth.
9. Place the dressing, salt and pepper over the salad and toss to combine.
10. Enjoy.

GLAZED
Radish Fruit Salad

Prep Time: 35 mins
Total Time: 35 mins

Servings per Recipe: 8
Calories   366.7
Fat   21.7g
Cholesterol   3.9mg
Sodium   202.6mg
Carbohydrates   45.9g
Protein   2.5g

Ingredients

2 carrots, grated
2 stalks celery, sliced
2 apples, grated
6 radishes, grated
1 C. raisins
1/2 C. chopped dates
1/2 C. chopped dried apricot
1/2 sliced almonds

1 C. plain yogurt
1/2 tsp salt
1/2 C. lemon juice
1/4 C. honey
3/4 C. oil
1 dash salt

Directions

1. In a bowl, add all the dried fruit, apples, vegetables and almonds and mix well.
2. In a second bowl, add the remaining ingredients and mix until well combined.
3. Place the dressing over the salad and toss to coat well.
4. Refrigerate to chill completely.
5. Enjoy chilled.

Fruit Salad Jakarta

Prep Time: 10 mins
Total Time: 10 mins

Servings per Recipe: 4
Calories	608.0
Fat	4.3g
Cholesterol	0.0mg
Sodium	1282.2mg
Carbohydrates	151.8g
Protein	3.5g

Ingredients

- 2 C. honey
- 2 tbsp peanut butter
- 1 tsp vinegar
- 2 tsp salt
- 2 tsp red peppers
- 4 C. shredded carrots, apples, pears and cucumbers

Directions

1. In a bowl, add the vinegar, peanut butter, honey, salt and pepper and mix until well combined.
2. Add the fruit and vegetables and gently, stir to combine.
3. Place in the fridge for about 2 hours.
4. Enjoy chilled.

SEATTLE
Creamy Quinoa Salad

Prep Time: 5 mins
Total Time: 20 mins

Servings per Recipe: 6
Calories   169.1
Fat   1.9g
Cholesterol   0.0mg
Sodium   108.6mg
Carbohydrates   35.3g
Protein   4.6g

Ingredients

1/4 tsp salt
1 C. quinoa, rinsed
1/3 C. chopped mint
1/4 C. nonfat vanilla yogurt
2 tbsp orange juice
1 1/2 C. sliced strawberries
2 kiwi fruits, peeled and sliced
1 (11 oz.) cans mandarin orange sections, drained

Directions

1. In a pot, add 2 C. of the water and salt and cook until boiling.
2. Add the quinoa and stir to combine.
3. Set the heat to low and cook, covered for about 15 minutes.
4. Meanwhile, in a food processor, add the yogurt, orange juice and mint and pulse until smooth.
5. Reserve some kiwi and strawberry slices for topping.
6. In a bowl, add the quinoa, fruit and yogurt sauce and gently, toss to combine.
7. Top with the reserved fruit slices and place in the fridge for about refrigerate 3 hours.
8. Enjoy chilled.

2nd Grade
Fruit Salad

🥣 Prep Time: 20 mins
🕐 Total Time: 25 mins

Servings per Recipe: 4
Calories 49.7
Fat 0.0g
Cholesterol 0.0mg
Sodium 1.5mg
Carbohydrates 12.4g
Protein 0.0g

Ingredients

- 6 C. cut-up fruit
- 1 C. water
- 3 tbsp sugar
- 4 tsp cornstarch
- 1 1/2 tbsp fresh lemon juice
- 1/2 tsp lemon, zest
- 1/2 tsp vanilla

Directions

1. In a bowl, add the fruit and mix well.
2. In a pot, add the cornstarch, sugar and lemon juice and mix until the cornstarch is dissolved.
3. Place the pan over medium heat and cook until boiling, mixing continuously.
4. Cook for about 1 minute, mixing continuously.
5. Remove from the heat and stir in the vanilla and lemon zest.
6. Keep aside to cool for about 20 minutes.
7. Place the sauce over fruit and stir to combine well.
8. Refrigerate to chill completely.
9. Enjoy chilled.

CARIBBEAN
Honeydew and Guava Salad

Prep Time: 20 mins
Total Time: 20 mins

Servings per Recipe: 6
Calories 181.2
Fat 0.9g
Cholesterol 0.0mg
Sodium 22.6mg
Carbohydrates 44.8g
Protein 3.2g

Ingredients

1/2 honeydew melon, peeled, seeded and sliced
1/4 watermelon, peeled, seeded and sliced
2 guavas, seeded and sliced
3 nectarines, peeled and sliced
18 strawberries, hulled and sliced
1 dash of toasted coconut
strained yogurt

Syrup
3 tbsp sugar
2/3 C. water
1 cinnamon stick
4 cardamom pods, crushed
1 clove
1 orange, juice
1 lime, juice

Directions

1. For the syrup: in a bowl, add the water, sugar and cook until boiling, mixing continuously.
2. Cook for about 2 minutes, mixing continuously.
3. Remove from the heat and stir in the lime and orange juice.
4. In a bowl, add the fruit and mix.
5. Through a strainer, strain the cooked syrup over fruit.
6. Enjoy with a topping of the coconut alongside the strained yogurt.

5-Ingredient Chinese Salad

Prep Time: 20 mins
Total Time: 1 hr 20 mins

Servings per Recipe: 6
Calories   190.0
Fat   16.0g
Cholesterol   33.7mg
Sodium   41.0mg
Carbohydrates   10.1g
Protein   2.5g

Ingredients

- 2 C. sour cream
- 2 tbsp honey
- 1 tbsp orange juice concentrate
- 1 tsp lemon zest
- 6 C. fruit, chopped

Directions

1. For the sauce: in a bowl, add all the ingredients except the fruit and mix until well combined.
2. Cover the bowl and place in the fridge for about 2 hours.
3. Add the fruit and gently, stir to combine.
4. Enjoy.

MEMPHIS INSPIRED
Fruit Salad

Prep Time: 20 mins
Total Time: 3 hrs 20 mins

Servings per Recipe: 8
Calories   386.8
Fat   14.7g
Cholesterol   29.5mg
Sodium   116.1mg
Carbohydrates   61.9g
Protein   6.1g

Ingredients

1 (14 oz.) cans sweetened condensed milk
1 C. sour cream
1/2 C. lime juice
1 (20 oz.) cans pineapple chunks, drained
1 (11 oz.) cans mandarin orange segments, drained
1 1/2 C. grapes, halved
1 medium banana, sliced
1 C. sweetened flaked coconut
1 C. miniature marshmallow, optional
1/2 C. maraschino cherry, halved, well-drained & patted dry
1/2 C. nuts, chopped

Directions

1. In a bowl, add the sour cream, condensed milk and lime juice and stir to combine well.
2. Add the remaining ingredients except the cherries and nuts and stir to combine.
3. Cover the bowl and place in the fridge for about 8-12 hours.
4. Add the cherries and gently, sir to combine.
5. Enjoy with a toping of the nuts.

Mi Tia's Fruit Salad

Prep Time: 10 mins
Total Time: 10 mins

Servings per Recipe: 6
Calories	196.3
Fat	6.2g
Cholesterol	3.7mg
Sodium	19.8mg
Carbohydrates	32.3g
Protein	5.0g

Ingredients

- 6 oz. vanilla yogurt
- 1 C. crunchy granola cereal
- 2 kiwi fruits, chopped
- 1 pear, chopped
- 1 plum, chopped
- 1 granny smith apple, chopped
- 1/2 C. strawberry, chopped
- 1/4 C. blueberries
- 1/2 C. blackberry
- 1/4 tsp cinnamon
- 1/4 C. raisins

Directions

1. In a bowl, add all the ingredients and mix well.
2. Enjoy.

SWEET BALSAMIC
Dates Salad

Prep Time: 15 mins
Total Time: 15 mins

Servings per Recipe: 4
Calories	149.8
Fat	0.2g
Cholesterol	0.0mg
Sodium	11.9mg
Carbohydrates	39.1g
Protein	1.5g

Ingredients

1 (6 oz.) cans pineapple chunks, drained
3 oz. pitted dates
1 medium carrot, sliced
1 orange, peeled and sliced
1 banana, peeled and sliced
3 tsp honey

3 tsp white balsamic vinegar
2 tsp lime juice
1 tsp lime zest

Directions

1. In a bowl, add the dates, orange, pineapple and carrot and mix well.
2. In another bowl, add the honey, lime zest, lime juice and vinegar and beat until well combined.
3. Place the dressing over the salad and toss to coat well.
4. Refrigerate to chill completely.
5. Enjoy chilled.

Blackberry Raspberry Salad

Prep Time: 15 mins
Total Time: 27 mins

Servings per Recipe: 8
Calories   256.0
Fat   6.1g
Cholesterol   0.0mg
Sodium   23.1mg
Carbohydrates   50.2g
Protein   3.5g

Ingredients

- 1 1/4 C. divided sugar
- 2 tbsp lemon juice
- 2 tsp granted lemon zest
- 1 C. sliced almonds
- 1 tsp dry ginger
- 1 pinch salt
- 1 pint blackberry
- 1 pint raspberries
- 2 1/2 inches Granny Smith apples, sliced, cored, quartered, and cut
- 1 pint sorbet
- 1/4 C. small basil leaves

Directions

1. For the syrup: in a pot, add 1/2 C. of the sugar and 1/2 C. of the water and cook for about 3 minutes, stirring continuously.
2. Remove from the heat and transfer the syrup into a bowl.
3. Add the lemon zest and juice and stir to combine.
4. Place in the fridge until using.
5. For the almond brittle: in a pan, add the remaining 3/4 C. of the sugar and enough water to wet the sugar over medium heat and cook for about 6-8 minutes, stirring frequently.
6. Add the almonds and stir to combine with the sugar mixture evenly.
7. Stir in the ginger and a pinch salt and remove from the heat.
8. Immediately, place the almonds onto a baking sheet and keep aside to cool completely.
9. Then, break the almond brittle into bite size pieces.
10. In a bowl, add the apple slices, raspberries, blackberries and sugar syrup and toss to coat well.
11. Place in the fridge to chill completely.
12. Enjoy with a topping of the raspberry sorbet, almonds brittle and basil leaves.

FRUIT SALAD
Minnetonka

Prep Time: 10 mins
Total Time: 10 mins

Servings per Recipe: 4
Calories	122.9
Fat	0.2g
Cholesterol	0.0mg
Sodium	3.7mg
Carbohydrates	30.4g
Protein	1.7g

Ingredients

1/4 C. Orange Marmalade
3 tbsp Caramel Topping
1/4 tsp cinnamon

2 C. mixed fruit, chopped

Directions

1. In a bowl, add the caramel topping, marmalade and cinnamon and mix well.
2. Add the fruit and gently, stir to combine.
3. Enjoy.

Maui Pineapple Salad

Prep Time: 10 mins
Total Time: 10 mins

Servings per Recipe: 4
Calories	254.4
Fat	14.6g
Cholesterol	22.4mg
Sodium	157.4mg
Carbohydrates	25.9g
Protein	7.5g

Ingredients

- 7 oz. pineapple chunks, drained
- 4 oz. mandarin oranges, can drained
- 7 oz. tropical fruit salad, drained
- 2 oz. coconut milk
- 4 oz. goat cheese
- 1/4 C. toasted coconut

Directions

1. In a bowl, add all the ingredients except the coconut and mix well.
2. Refrigerate to chill completely.
3. Enjoy with a topping of the coconut.

FRUIT SALAD
with the Works (Plums, Grapes, Figs, Lemon)

Prep Time: 10 mins
Total Time: 13 mins

Servings per Recipe: 4
Calories   111.6
Fat   1.5g
Cholesterol   0.0mg
Sodium   585.4mg
Carbohydrates   26.4g
Protein   1.5g

Ingredients

1 1/2 C. purple grapes, halved
2 purple plums
1/4 C. shopped radicchio lettuce
1 small onion, sliced rounds
3 tbsp dried goji berries
6 dried figs, de-stemmed, sliced
1 Meyer lemon, juiced
1 tbsp vegan mayonnaise
1 tsp oil
1 tsp course sea salt
1 tsp agave syrup

Directions

1. In a wok, add the oil and cook until heated through.
2. Add the fig slices and stir fry for about 4-5 minutes.
3. In a bowl, add the fig slices and remaining ingredients and mix until well combined.
4. Enjoy.

Simple Ceviche Formulae

Prep Time: 20 mins
Total Time: 20 mins

Servings per Recipe: 6
Calories   335.5
Fat   11.2g
Cholesterol   95.5mg
Sodium   859.0mg
Carbohydrates   0.8g
Protein   53.8g

Ingredients

- 3 lbs. boneless white fish, skinless, cubed
- lime juice
- orange juice
- 2 tbsp white vinegar
- kosher salt & ground black pepper
- 2 tbsp olive oil
- 1/4 small red onion, chopped
- 3 green onions, trimmed and chopped
- 1 celery rib, chopped
- 2 tbsp cilantro, chopped

Directions

1. Get a mixing bowl: Stir in it the fish with the juice of 2 limes.
2. Chill it in the fridge for 16 min.
3. Get a mixing bowl: Whisk in it the juice of 1 lime, orange juice, vinegar, salt, pepper, and olive oil.
4. Drain the fish and add it with onion, green onion, celery, and cilantro. Toss them to coat.
5. Chill the ceviche in the fridge for 3 h then serve it.
6. Enjoy.

FULL BARCELONA
Ceviche

Prep Time: 10 mins
Total Time: 4 hrs 10 mins

Servings per Recipe: 8
Calories 122.7
Fat 2.8g
Cholesterol 130.6mg
Sodium 340.1mg
Carbohydrates 8.7g
Protein 16.1g

Ingredients

1/2 lb. shrimp, peeled and deveined
1/2 lb. squid, cleaned and sliced into rings
1/2 lb. scallops, quartered if large
1 (10 oz.) cans Rotel Tomatoes, drained
2 medium ripe tomatoes, seeded and diced
1/2 large cucumber, peeled and diced
1/2 large green pepper, diced
1/2 medium red sweet onion, diced
1/2 C. chopped fresh cilantro

1 tsp minced garlic
3/4 C. lime juice
1/2 tsp cumin
1 tbsp capers, chopped
1/2 C. hot and spicy hot V8
1 tbsp extra virgin olive oil
1 tsp Accent seasoning
salt & pepper

Directions

1. Place a large saucepan of salted water over high heat. Bring it to a boil.
2. Cook in it the shrimp for 1 min. Drain it and place it in a bowl of ice-cold water.
3. Drain it and chop it. Place it aside.
4. Cook the squid in the same saucepan for 10 sec. Drain it, stir it into the cold water and drain it again.
5. Repeat the process with scallops cooking them for 60 sec.
6. Get a mixing bowl: Stir in it the scallops with shrimp, squid, and lime juice.
7. Cover the bowl and place it in the fridge for 60 min.
8. Once the time is up, stir the remaining ingredients into the seafood bowl. Toss them to coat.
9. Chill it in the fridge for 4 h then serve it.
10. Enjoy.

Ferdinand's Favorite

Prep Time: 2 hrs 15 mins
Total Time: 2 hrs 15 mins

Servings per Recipe: 24
Calories   29.8
Fat   2.2g
Cholesterol   1.2mg
Sodium   39.5mg
Carbohydrates   2.5g
Protein   0.2g

Ingredients

2 C. white fish fillets
1/2 C. lime juice, strained
1 C. carrot, cooked and cut into strips
1 C. tomatoes, peeled and chopped
1/2 C. green onion, chopped
1/3 C. cilantro, chopped
1 tbsp olive oil
2 tbsp white vinegar
salt
pepper
1/4 C. water
1/2 C. mayonnaise
corn chips
chopped lettuce

Directions

1. Get a mixing bowl: Stir in it the lime juice with fish. Cover it and place it in the fridge for 60 min.
2. Once the time is up, drain it and transfer it to a mixing bowl.
3. Add to it the carrots, tomatoes, onions, cilantro, oil, and vinegar.
4. Season them with a pinch of salt and pepper. Toss them to coat.
5. Use a plastic wrap to cover the bowl and chill it in the fridge for 60 min.
6. Once the time is up, stir in the mayo then serve your ceviche right away.
7. Enjoy.

HOT HAWAIIAN
Ceviche

🍳 Prep Time: 30 mins
🕐 Total Time: 45 mins

Servings per Recipe: 4
Calories 171.6
Fat 15.4g
Cholesterol 0.0mg
Sodium 37.1mg
Carbohydrates 9.4g
Protein 2.4g

Ingredients

10 oz. coconut milk
2 tbsp chopped ginger
2 tbsp grated horseradish
3 jalapeno peppers, seeded and minced
3 tbsp chopped cilantro
1 lime, juice

12 oz. sashimi-grade tuna, cubed
1 tomatoes, seeded and diced
1 small red onion, julienned
1 scallion, julienned

Directions

1. Place a large saucepan over medium heat. Stir in it the coconut milk, ginger, and horseradish.
2. Bring them to a rolling boil. Let them cook until they reduce by 1/4.
3. Once the time is up, strain the milk sauce and discard the solids.
4. Get a mixing bowl: Stir in it the tuna, tomato, jalapeno, cilantro, lime juice and coconut sauce.
5. Adjust the seasoning of your ceviche then places it in the fridge until ready to serve.
6. Enjoy.

Imitation Ceviche

Prep Time: 10 mins
Total Time: 10 mins

Servings per Recipe: 4
Calories	110.3
Fat	1.2g
Cholesterol	16.9mg
Sodium	1587.3mg
Carbohydrates	14.4g
Protein	11.3g

Ingredients

- 1 (12 oz.) packages flaked krab imitation crabmeat, chopped
- 1 (10 oz.) cans diced tomatoes with green chilies, drained
- 6 red radishes, small diced
- 1 bunch green onion, sliced
- 1 to 2 lime, juice
- 1 tsp salt
- hot sauce

Directions

1. Get a mixing bowl: Stir in it all the ingredients.
2. Place it in the fridge and let it chill for at least 2 h.
3. Serve your ceviche with some chips or tostadas.
4. Enjoy.

ARIZONA
Shrimp Ceviche

Prep Time: 45 mins
Total Time: 50 mins

Servings per Recipe: 6
Calories	335.0
Fat	8.5g
Cholesterol	345.6mg
Sodium	641.3mg
Carbohydrates	17.8g
Protein	46.9g

Ingredients

- 3 lbs. small shrimp
- 1 bunch coriander
- 2 red onions, sliced
- 1 jalapeno pepper, chopped
- 10 lemons, juice
- 2 tbsp olive oil
- 4 tbsp tomato sauce
- 1/2 C. Worcestershire sauce
- 1 pinch salt

Directions

1. Place a heavy saucepan over medium heat. Stir in it the water with Worcestershire sauce and salt.
2. Bring them to a boil. Stir in the shrimp and cook it for 3 min. Drain it and chop it.
3. Get a mixing bowl: Stir in it the shrimp with coriander, onions, lemon juice, jalapeno pepper to taste, tomato sauce and olive oil.
4. Adjust the seasoning of your ceviche then chill it in the fridge for 10 min. Serve it with some crackers.
5. Enjoy.

Southern Sole Ceviche

Prep Time: 30 mins
Total Time: 24 hrs 30 mins

Servings per Recipe: 6
Calories	403.0
Fat	37.6g
Cholesterol	34.0mg
Sodium	350.5mg
Carbohydrates	7.9g
Protein	10.2g

Ingredients

- 1 lb. sole fillet, cubed
- 1 C. salad oil
- 1/4 C. chopped cilantro
- 1 C. sliced pimento-stuffed green olives
- 2 C. minced onions
- 2/3 C. lime juice
- 2 garlic cloves, minced
- 2 bay leaves
- 2 -3 pickled jalapeno peppers, minced
- salt and pepper
- lettuce and sliced celery

Directions

1. Get a mixing bowl: Stir in it all the ingredients.
2. Layover it a plastic wrap to cover it. Chill it in the fridge for 14 to 24 h.
3. Once the time is up, discard the bay leaves. Serve your ceviche with some lettuce.
4. Enjoy.

SPICED Kale Ceviche

Prep Time: 10 mins
Total Time: 10 mins

Servings per Recipe: 6
Calories 117.8
Fat 6.3g
Cholesterol 0.0mg
Sodium 121.6mg
Carbohydrates 15.7g
Protein 2.6g

Ingredients

1 bunch kale, leaves
1 large avocado, peeled
1 tbsp lemon juice
1/4 tsp salt
1/2 tsp crushed red pepper flakes
1/2 red bell pepper

1 small carrot, grated
1/2 purple onion, chopped
1 1/2 C. mandarin orange segments

Directions

1. Get a mixing bowl: Toss in it the kale with avocado, lemon juice, salt and red pepper flakes.
2. Mix them well with your hands until they avocado become mashed and smooth.
3. Add the rest of the ingredients. Toss them to coat.
4. Chill your ceviche in the fridge for 35 min then serve it.
5. Enjoy.

Ceviche Cups

Prep Time: 10 mins
Total Time: 10 mins

Servings per Recipe: 4
Calories	278.8
Fat	15.1g
Cholesterol	37.4mg
Sodium	346.6mg
Carbohydrates	15.1g
Protein	23.6g

Ingredients

- 2 (6 oz.) cans albacore tuna in water, drained
- 1/2 C. sweet onion, diced
- 1 large tomatoes, seeded and diced
- 1 small cucumber, peeled and diced
- 1/4 C. cilantro,
- 1 - 2 serrano chili, diced
- 2 - 3 limes, juice
- 1 tbsp olive oil
- salt
- pepper
- 1 large avocado, diced
- 8 tostadas

Directions

1. Get a mixing bowl: Stir in it the tuna, onion, tomato, cucumber, and cilantro.
2. Pour over them the lime juice, olive oil, salt, and pepper. Toss them to coat.
3. Stir in the serrano chilies, followed by avocado.
4. Spoon your ceviche into tostadas then serve them right away.
5. Enjoy.

BOARDWALK
Ceviche

Prep Time: 20 mins
Total Time: 2 hrs 20 mins

Servings per Recipe: 20
Calories	171.7
Fat	2.0g
Cholesterol	68.6mg
Sodium	1177.8mg
Carbohydrates	11.7g
Protein	26.8g

Ingredients

5 tomatoes, peeled and diced
1 onion, Red, diced
6 lb. halibut, cubed
32 oz. lime juice
2 C. Clamato juice
2/3 C. ketchup
2 oz. sugar
1.5 oz. salt
1 English cucumber, seeded and cubed
1 bunch cilantro

Directions

1. Get a mixing bowl: Stir in it the cucumber, onion, tomato, and halibut.
2. Add the lime juice with clamato juice and ketchup. Toss them to coat.
3. Cover the bowl with a plastic wrap and refrigerate it for 2 h.
4. Once the time is up, serve your ceviche with some chips.
5. Enjoy.

Wednesday's
Lunch Ceviche

Prep Time: 15 mins
Total Time: 15 mins

Servings per Recipe: 4
Calories	689.3
Fat	28.5g
Cholesterol	32.3mg
Sodium	92.8mg
Carbohydrates	89.0g
Protein	22.9g

Ingredients

3/4 lb. tuna, filets
2 tomatoes, diced
1 green pepper, seeded and diced
1 - 3 hot red chili pepper, diced
1/2 C. cucumber, peeled, seeded and diced
1 C. lime juice
2 C. coconut milk
salt & pepper

Directions

1. Get a mixing bowl: Stir in it all the ingredients.
2. Cover the bowl and chill it in the fridge for at least 2 h.
3. Once the time is up, adjust the seasoning of your ceviche then serve it.
4. Enjoy.

LOUISIANA
Ceviche

Prep Time: 1 hr
Total Time: 5 hrs

Servings per Recipe: 6
Calories   207.6
Fat   14.0g
Cholesterol   41.5mg
Sodium   467.1mg
Carbohydrates   9.3g
Protein   12.8g

Ingredients

1 lb. catfish fillet, cut into pieces
1 tsp grated lemon zest
1/2 C. lemon juice
1 tsp grated lime zest
1/2 C. lime juice
2 tbsp extra-virgin olive oil
1 C. seeded diced ripe tomatoes
1/2 C. diced red onion
2 garlic cloves, sliced

2 tbsp cilantro leaves
1 tbsp oregano leaves
1 jalapeno pepper, seeded, deveined, and minced
1 tsp salt
1/2 tsp sugar
1 avocado, pitted, peeled, and diced

Directions

1. Get a Ziploc bag; stir in it the fish with lemon and lime zest and juices.
2. Seal the bag and shake it to coat. Place it in the fridge for 5 h to 18 h.
3. Once the time is up, drain the fish and transfer it to a mixing bowl.
4. Add to it the rest of the ingredients and toss them to coat. Serve it with some crackers.
5. Enjoy.

Catalina's
Cabbage Ceviche

🥣 Prep Time: 30 mins
🕐 Total Time: 31 mins

Servings per Recipe: 12
Calories 108.7
Fat 1.0g
Cholesterol 79.6mg
Sodium 378.1mg
Carbohydrates 15.8g
Protein 11.3g

Ingredients

1 head green cabbage, shredded
6 small English cucumbers, shredded
1 large onion,
1 yellow pepper, shredded
4 large garlic cloves, crushed and mashed with 1 tsp. salt
4 tomatoes, seeded and chopped
4 large limes, juice
1 C. cilantro,
salt and pepper
1 lb. shrimp, peeled and deveined

Directions

1. Bring a large saucepan of water to a boil. Cook in it the shrimp for 2 min.
2. Drain it and chop it.
3. Get a baking dish: Stir in it all the ingredients including the chopped shrimp.
4. cover the bowl and place it in the fridge for 30 min. Serve it with some chips.
5. Enjoy.

WEST INDIAN
Ceviche

Prep Time: 40 mins
Total Time: 42 mins

Servings per Recipe: 4
Calories 470.4
Fat 13.0g
Cholesterol 265.0mg
Sodium 1131.5mg
Carbohydrates 61.3g
Protein 42.5g

Ingredients

1/2 lb. salmon, cubed
1 lb. of shell-less shrimp
1 big mango, peeled and diced
1/2 red onion, diced
4 small tomatoes, peeled and diced
1 chile serrano pepper, chopped

cilantro, to desire
1 avocado, diced
20 limes, juice

Directions

1. Get a mixing bowl: Stir in it the shrimp and salmon with lime juice. Season them with a pinch of salt.
2. Cover the bowl and place it in the fridge for 2 h 30 min.
3. Once the time is up, drain the shrimp and salmon. Transfer them to another mixing bowl.
4. Add the remaining ingredients and toss them to coat.
5. Spoon your ceviche into serving glasses and serve them.
6. Enjoy.

Bahamian Ceviche

Prep Time: 20 mins
Total Time: 20 mins

Servings per Recipe: 6	
Calories	233.2
Fat	18.6g
Cholesterol	27.5mg
Sodium	69.5mg
Carbohydrates	5.4g
Protein	11.7g

Ingredients

- 2 C. conch, cleaned and diced
- 2 C. diced poached spiny lobsters
- 1/2 small red onion, diced
- 3 scallions, sliced on the diagonal
- 1/2 small red pepper, diced
- 1/2 small yellow pepper, diced
- 1/2 small green pepper, diced
- 1/2 small papaya, peeled, seeded and diced
- 2 - 4 jalapenos, chopped
- 1/2 bunch chopped cilantro
- 1/2 bunch chopped basil
- 1/2 bunch chopped mint leaves
- 1 tbsp grated fresh ginger
- 1/2 lime, juiced
- 1/4 C. rice wine vinegar
- 1/2 C. extra virgin olive oil
- salt and pepper
- 1 pinch ground habanero chile pepper

Directions

1. Get a mixing bowl: Stir in it all the ingredients.
2. Cover it and chill it in the fridge for 3 h 30 min.
3. Once the time is up, spoon your ceviche into serving glasses. Serve them with some chips.
4. Enjoy.

NEW ENGLAND
Ceviche Bowls

Prep Time: 3 hrs
Total Time: 3 hrs

Servings per Recipe: 4
Calories   153.3
Fat   4.5g
Cholesterol   34.0mg
Sodium   682.2mg
Carbohydrates   10.6g
Protein   17.1g

Ingredients

1 lb. clams, cleaned and chopped
1 pink grapefruit, peeled and diced
1 tsp pink peppercorns
12 mint leaves, slivered

1 tbsp extra virgin olive oil
kosher salt
tortilla chips

Directions

1. Get a mixing bowl: Stir in it all the ingredients.
2. Cover the bowl and place it in the fridge for 3 to 4 h.
3. Once the time is up, adjust the seasoning of your ceviche then serve it.
4. Enjoy.

Sunday's Ceviche

Prep Time: 15 mins
Total Time: 25 mins

Servings per Recipe: 4
Calories   236.9
Fat   10.8g
Cholesterol   56.7mg
Sodium   344.3mg
Carbohydrates   13.4g
Protein   25.0g

Ingredients

- 1 lb. tilapia fillet, cut into pieces
- 1 - 2 jalapeno pepper, minced
- 1/2 C. lime juice
- 1/2 C. fresh cilantro, chopped and divided
- 1 tsp fresh oregano, chopped
- 1/4 tsp salt
- 1 large green bell pepper, halved crosswise and sliced
- 1 large tomatoes, chopped
- 1/2 C. white onion, sliced
- 1/4 C. green olives, quartered
- 1 avocado, chopped

Directions

1. Place a pan over high heat. Place in it the fish and cover it with water. Cook it until it starts boiling.
2. Turn off the heat and cover the pan. Let the fish sit for 6 min.
3. Get a mixing bowl: Stir in it the fish after draining it with bell pepper, tomato, onion, and olives.
4. Cover the bowl and chill it in the fridge for 25 min.
5. Once the time is up, add the rest of the avocado and cilantro.
6. Adjust the seasoning of your ceviche then serve it.
7. Enjoy.

ISABELLE'S
Ceviche

Prep Time: 3 hrs
Total Time: 3 hrs

Servings per Recipe: 4
Calories   341.7
Fat   4.9g
Cholesterol   179.5mg
Sodium   290.3mg
Carbohydrates   30.3g
Protein   44.8g

Ingredients

2/3 lb. large shrimp, peeled and cleaned
2/3 lb. scallops, quartered
2/3 lb. salmon, skinned and pin-boned
1 tomatoes, chopped
1 mango, peeled and cubed
1/4 red onion, chopped
1 jalapeno, seeded and
1 C. lime juice
2/3 C. orange juice

1/2 C. loosely packed coriander leaves, chopped
1 tbsp powdered sugar
1 large oranges, peeled and segmented
popcorn, seasoned with chili, cumin, and salt

Directions

1. Bring a salted saucepan of water to a boil. Cook in it the shrimp for 1 min.
2. Drain it and transfer it to an ice bowl of water. Drain it again and transfer it to a mixing bowl.
3. Add to them the scallops with salmon, mango, onion, chile, lime and orange juice.
4. Cover the bowl and place it in the fridge for 3 h 30 min.
5. Once the time is up, drain the fish and transfer it to a mixing bowl.
6. Stir into them coriander, sugar, orange, and a pinch of salt. Serve your ceviche right away.
7. Enjoy.

Peruvian Salad Dressing (Cilantro Based)

Prep Time:	25 mins
Total Time:	25 mins

Servings per Recipe:	32
Calories	42 kcal
Fat	4.1 g
Carbohydrates	1.6 g
Protein	< 0.3 g
Cholesterol	< 0 mg
Sodium	2 mg

Ingredients

1/3 C. olive oil
1 clove garlic, minced
3/4 C. diced fresh cilantro
2 avocados, peeled, seeded and cubed
1 large cucumber, peeled, seeded and cut into chunks

1/4 C. lemon juice
salt and pepper to taste

Directions

1. Puree all the ingredients in a food processor for 1 min while pouring in the olive oil.
2. Once all the oil has been adding continue to puree the dressing for another 60 secs.
3. Add in some pepper and salt then pulse the dressing a few more times until it is smooth.
4. Enjoy chilled.

SIMPLE
Pesto

Prep Time: 2 mins
Total Time: 12 mins

Servings per Recipe: 6
Calories	199 kcal
Fat	21.1 g
Carbohydrates	2g
Protein	1.7 g
Cholesterol	0 mg
Sodium	389 mg

Ingredients

1/4 C. almonds
3 cloves garlic
1 1/2 C. fresh basil leaves
1/2 C. olive oil
1 pinch ground nutmeg
salt and pepper to taste

Directions

1. Set your oven to 450 degrees F before doing anything else.
2. Arrange the almonds onto a cookie sheet and bake for about 10 minutes or till toasted slightly.
3. In a food processor, add the toasted almonds and the remaining ingredients till a rough paste forms.

How to Make Hummus

Prep Time: 10 mins
Total Time: 10 mins

Servings per Recipe: 16
Calories	77 kcal
Fat	4.3 g
Carbohydrates	8.1g
Protein	2.6 g
Cholesterol	0 mg
Sodium	236 mg

Ingredients

- 2 C. canned garbanzo beans, drained
- 1/3 C. tahini
- 1/4 C. lemon juice
- 1 tsp salt
- 2 cloves garlic, halved
- 1 tbsp olive oil
- 1 pinch paprika
- 1 tsp minced fresh parsley

Directions

1. Blend the following in a food processer until paste-like: garlic, garbanzos, salt, tahini, and lemon juice.
2. Add this to a bowl with olive oil, paprika, and parsley.
3. Enjoy.

MEDITERRANEAN
Red Hummus

Prep Time: 15 mins
Total Time: 1 hr 15 mins

Servings per Recipe: 8	
Calories	64 kcal
Fat	2.2 g
Carbohydrates	9.6g
Protein	2.5 g
Cholesterol	0 mg
Sodium	370 mg

Ingredients

1 (15 oz.) can garbanzo beans, drained
1 (4 oz.) jar roasted red peppers
3 tbsps lemon juice
1 1/2 tbsps tahini
1 clove garlic, minced
1/2 tsp ground cumin
1/2 tsp cayenne pepper
1/4 tsp salt
1 tbsp chopped fresh parsley

Directions

1. Blend the following until smooth: salt, chickpeas, cayenne, red peppers, cumin, lemon juice, garlic, and tahini.
2. Add everything to a bowl and place a covering of plastic over it.
3. Now place it all in the fridge for 60 mins.
4. Before serving the mix top the hummus with parsley.
5. Enjoy.

Black Bean Hummus

Prep Time: 5 mins
Total Time: 5 mins

Servings per Recipe: 8
Calories	81 kcal
Fat	3.1 g
Carbohydrates	10.3 g
Protein	3.9 g
Cholesterol	0 mg
Sodium	427 mg

Ingredients

- 1 clove garlic
- 1 (15 oz.) can black beans; drain and reserve liquid
- 2 tbsps lemon juice
- 1 1/2 tbsps tahini
- 3/4 tsp ground cumin
- 1/2 tsp salt
- 1/4 tsp cayenne pepper
- 1/4 tsp paprika
- 10 Greek olives

Directions

1. Blend your garlic in a blender with a few pulses to mince it then add in: half of your cayenne, black beans, salt, 2 tbsps of black bean juice, half tsp cumin, tahini, and lemon juice.
2. Blend this mix until it has the consistency of hummus.
3. Add everything to a bowl and top it all with olives and paprika.
4. Enjoy.

MESA MEDITERRANEAN
Chicken Wraps

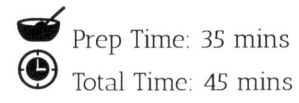

Prep Time: 35 mins
Total Time: 45 mins

Servings per Recipe: 2
Calories	1169.8
Fat	51.3g
Cholesterol	169.4mg
Sodium	1654.5mg
Carbohydrates	108.5g
Protein	69.1g

Ingredients

4 boneless skinless chicken breasts
2 garlic cloves, crushed
1/4 tsp ground cinnamon
1 tsp ground allspice
1/2 tsp black pepper
1 tbsp olive oil
3 tbsp lemon juice
2 tbsp plain yogurt
Wraps
4 pita bread

shredded lettuce
2 - 3 tomatoes, sliced
6 - 8 radishes, sliced
Spicy Mayo
1 C. mayonnaise
1 green chile, seeded and chopped
1 tbsp chopped coriander
1 tbsp lime juice

Directions

1. Slice the breasts into 3 slices. Get a large mixing bowl: Mix in it the garlic, cinnamon, allspice, pepper, oil, lemon juice, and yogurt.
2. Stir in the chicken slices to coat them with the mixture. Put on the lid and place it in the fridge for 1 h. Before you do anything else, preheat the grill and grease it. Press the chicken strips onto skewers. Grill them for 4 to 6 min on each side until they are done.
3. Get a mixing bowl: Whisk in it the mayo with chile, coriander, and lime juice. Open the pita bread. Arrange in them the grilled chicken followed by lettuce, tomato, radishes, and chili mayo.
4. Season them with some salt and pepper. Serve your chicken wraps immediately.
5. Enjoy.

Trinidad Rotisserie Wraps

🥣 Prep Time: 15 mins
🕐 Total Time: 15 mins

Servings per Recipe: 2
Calories   157.7
Fat   12.9g
Cholesterol   0.0mg
Sodium   5.1mg
Carbohydrates   11.0g
Protein   2.3g

Ingredients

- 1 1/2 C. rotisserie chicken, cold and chopped
- 1/2 C. fresh mango, diced
- 1/4 C. green onion, sliced
- 1/4 C. red bell pepper, diced
- 1/4 C. macadamia nuts, chopped
- 1/4 C. cilantro lime salad dressing, see appendix
- 6 - 8 butter lettuce leaves

Directions

1. Get a mixing bowl: Toss in it the chicken with mango, green onion, bell pepper, macadamia nuts, and cilantro dressing.
2. Divide the mixture between the lettuce leaves then serve them.
3. Enjoy.

MEXICANA
Wraps

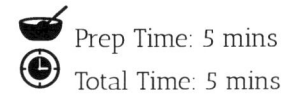

Prep Time: 5 mins
Total Time: 5 mins

Servings per Recipe: 1	
Calories	254.5
Fat	6.5g
Cholesterol	7.4mg
Sodium	749.2mg
Carbohydrates	36.8g
Protein	11.2g

Ingredients

1 tortilla, wrap
1 (3/4 oz.) wedge swiss cheese
2 thick roasted red peppers

Directions

1. Place a small pan over medium heat. Heat in it the bell pepper for 1 min.
2. Place a tortilla on a serving plate. Spread over it the swiss cheese.
3. Arrange the roasted pepper slices on top. Roll the tortilla over it tightly then serve it.
4. Enjoy.

Trinidad Pesto Wraps

Prep Time: 5 mins
Total Time: 5 mins

Servings per Recipe: 1
Calories	461.0
Fat	14.1g
Cholesterol	14.8mg
Sodium	835.2mg
Carbohydrates	69.0g
Protein	16.4g

Ingredients

- 1 large tortilla
- 2 tbsp basil pesto, see appendix
- 3 tbsp fat-free cream cheese
- 3 slices tomatoes
- 6 slices cucumbers
- 1/4 C. alfalfa sprout
- 2 tbsp shredded cheddar cheese
- 2 tbsp shredded carrots
- 4 slices deli turkey

Directions

1. Warm the tortilla in a pan for few seconds on each side. Transfer it to a plate.
2. Top it with pesto sauce, followed by cream cheese, tomato, cucumbers, alfalfa sprouts, carrot, turkey, and cheese.
3. Roll your tortilla burrito style then serve it.
4. Enjoy.

PICANTE BEAN Wraps

🍳 Prep Time: 20 mins
🕐 Total Time: 30 mins

Servings per Recipe: 2
Calories   871.9
Fat   19.9g
Cholesterol   37.7mg
Sodium   875.6mg
Carbohydrates   136.2g
Protein   36.5g

Ingredients

1 (15 1/2 oz.) cans black beans, drained
1/2 C. chopped red bell pepper
1/2 C. chopped yellow bell pepper
3/4 C. cooked long-grain white rice, warm
1/4 C. chopped cilantro
1/4 C. Picante sauce
1 tbsp hot adobo sauce
1/2 tsp ground cumin
3/4 C. shredded Monterey jack cheese
2 10-inch flour tortillas

Directions

1. Place a large saucepan over medium heat. Stir in it the beans for 4 min.
2. Stir in the bell peppers with rice, cilantro, Picante sauce, adobo sauce, cumin, a pinch of salt and pepper.
3. Spoon the mixture into the tortillas and spread them in an even layer.
4. Sprinkle the cheese on top then rolls them tightly. Slice your bean rolls in half then serve them.
5. Enjoy.

Mediterranean Cheese Wraps

Prep Time: 5 mins
Total Time: 5 mins

Servings per Recipe: 1
Calories   333.1
Fat   20.2g
Cholesterol   124.3mg
Sodium   2207.9mg
Carbohydrates   2.4g
Protein   33.4g

Ingredients

- 1 whole wheat sandwich wrap
- 2 oz. deli roast beef
- 1-oz chevre cheese
- 1 tsp light mayonnaise
- lettuce
- tomatoes

Directions

1. Heat the tortilla in the microwave for few seconds. Transfer it to a serving plate.
2. Top it with a layer of mayo, lettuce, tomato, roast beef, and goat cheese.
3. Roll your tortilla over the filling tightly then serve it.
4. Enjoy.

JAPANESE
Spring Roll Wraps

Prep Time: 20 mins
Total Time: 25 mins

Servings per Recipe: 1
Calories 187.8
Fat 9.1g
Cholesterol 23.0mg
Sodium 2054.0mg
Carbohydrates 4.9g
Protein 22.0g

Ingredients

4 rice paper sheets
25 g vermicelli rice noodles
100 g smoked salmon
1 tsp extra virgin olive oil
1 tbsp capers
2 medium mushrooms, diced
1/2 C. cabbage, diced
1 tbsp soy sauce
1 tbsp sweet chili sauce
1/4 tsp ground black pepper

Directions

1. Prepare the noodles by following the instructions on the package. Drain it.
2. Get a large mixing bowl: Mix in it the noodles with the rest of the ingredients except for the rice paper sheets.
3. Place the filling in the fridge for 12 min.
4. Place a rice sheet in some warm water for 2 min. Drain it and place it on a kitchen towel.
5. Spoon 1/4 of the filling on one side of it. Pull the sides of the sheet over the filling then roll it tightly.
6. Repeat the process with the remaining ingredients.
7. Serve your vermicelli Rolls immediately with your favorite dipping sauce.
8. Enjoy.

Dijon Genoa Wraps

Prep Time: 15 mins
Total Time: 15 mins

Servings per Recipe: 1
Calories   1104.3
Fat   63.6g
Cholesterol   47.2mg
Sodium   7971.9mg
Carbohydrates   101.4g
Protein   44.8g

Ingredients

- 1 tbsp cider vinegar
- salt
- pepper
- 1/2 medium red onion, sliced
- 2 small firm avocados, cut in wedges
- 4 large flour tortillas
- 4 oz. baby spring greens
- 6 oz. Genoa salami, sliced and cut into strips

Spread
- 3 tbsp Dijon mustard
- 2 tbsp balsamic vinegar
- 1/4 C. mayonnaise

Directions

1. Get a mixing bowl: Whisk in it the mustard with vinegar, and mayo.
2. Spread the mixture all over the tortillas leaving the sides empty.
3. Top them with a layer of onion, avocados, salami and spring onions.
4. Season them with some salt. Roll the tortilla over the filling tightly then serve them.
5. Enjoy.

PESTO Tilapia Lettuce Wraps

Prep Time: 20 mins
Total Time: 40 mins

Servings per Recipe: 2
Calories   3041.5
Fat   284.2g
Cholesterol   177.5mg
Sodium   2460.3mg
Carbohydrates   84.1g
Protein   54.8g

Ingredients

2 - 3 tilapia fillets
1 avocado, sliced
16 oz. canola oil
1 head iceberg lettuce
Batter
1 tsp Old Bay Seasoning
1 tsp salt
1 tsp black pepper
1 tsp cayenne pepper
1/2 tsp garlic powder
3/4 C. wheat flour
3/4 C. panko breadcrumbs

1 egg
1/2-1 C. water
Pesto
1/2 C. roasted red pepper
1/4 C. Greek yogurt
2 garlic cloves
1/2 C. bunch basil
1/2 C. parmesan and pecorino cheese blend
1/2 tsp pepper
1/4 C. olive oil

Directions

1. To prepare the batter:
2. Get a mixing bowl:: Mix in it the all the batter ingredients.
3. Cut each fish fillet into 3 pieces. Dip them completely in the batter.
4. Place a large deep pan over medium heat. Heat in it 3 inches of oil.
5. Deep fry in it the fish pieces until they become golden brown. Drain them and place them on paper towels to dry.
6. Get a food processor: Place in it all the pepper pesto ingredients. Season them with a pinch of salt. Blend them smooth.
7. Overlap each 2 lettuce leaves on a serving plate. Top them with fried fish followed by avocado and pepper pesto.
8. Serve your open wraps immediately.
9. Enjoy.

Bangkok Meets Morocco Wraps

Prep Time: 5 mins
Total Time: 15 mins

Servings per Recipe: 6
Calories   202.0
Fat   4.0g
Cholesterol   0.1mg
Sodium   615.5mg
Carbohydrates   34.9g
Protein   7.3g

Ingredients

- 2 (14 oz.) cans chickpeas, drained and rinsed
- 1 tbsp Thai style chili sauce or sriracha
- 2 tbsp hoisin sauce
- 1 tbsp low sodium soy sauce
- 1 tbsp olive oil
- 2 tbsp rice vinegar
- 1/2 tbsp sugar
- 1 tsp red pepper flakes
- 1 tbsp hot sauce
- 1/2 C. chopped basil
- 6 -8 lettuce leaves, Bibb

Directions

1. Get a blender: Place in it the chickpeas and pulse them several times until they become chunky.
2. Place a large skillet over medium heat. Heat in it 1 tbsp of olive oil.
3. Cook in it the chunky chickpeas for 4 min while stirring all the time.
4. Stir in the chili and hoisin sauce with soy sauce, rice vinegar, sugar, red pepper flakes, hot sauce, a pinch of salt and pepper.
5. Lower the heat and let them cook for 12 min. Stir in the basil leaves and cook them for 1 min.
6. Spoon the chickpea mixture into the lettuce wraps. Serve them right away.
7. Enjoy.

AMERICAN BACON Lettuce and Tomato Wraps

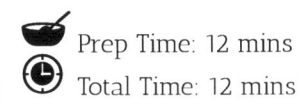

Prep Time: 12 mins
Total Time: 12 mins

Servings per Recipe: 4
Calories   451.4
Fat   22.2g
Cholesterol   41.5mg
Sodium   1133.9mg
Carbohydrates   39.9g
Protein   22.3g

Ingredients

3 C. romaine lettuce leaves, torn
1 medium tomatoes, chopped
1/3 C. turkey bacon, crisply cooked, crumbled
1/4 C. caesar salad dressing
1 1/2 C. Sargento artisan blends shredded parmesan cheese
4 (10 inches) flour tortillas

Directions

1. Get a mixing bowl: Stir in it the lettuce, tomato, bacon, salad dressing, and cheese.
2. Divide the mixture between the tortillas. Wrap them in the shape of burritos.
3. Serve your sandwiches immediately or refrigerate them until ready to serve.
4. Enjoy.

Guyanese Chickpea Wraps

🥣 Prep Time: 10 mins
🕐 Total Time: 1 hr 20 mins

Servings per Recipe: 8
Calories   200.6
Fat   6.7g
Cholesterol   0.0mg
Sodium   612.4mg
Carbohydrates   30.2g
Protein   6.2g

Ingredients

- 3 tbsp vegetable oil
- 2 C. onions, diced
- 5 garlic cloves, minced
- 1/2 chili pepper, seeded and diced
- fresh ginger, peeled and minced
- 3 tbsp curry powder
- 1 tsp ground cumin
- 1/4 tsp cayenne
- 1/4 tsp ground turmeric
- 1 tsp salt
- 2 (15 oz.) cans chickpeas, drained and rinsed
- whole wheat tortilla
- hot sauce
- red onion, diced
- cucumber, diced

Directions

1. Place a deep pan over medium heat. Heat in it the oil.
2. Cook in it the onion for 9 min. Stir in the garlic, chili pepper, and ginger. Cook them for 3 min.
3. Stir in the spices and cook them for 1 min. Stir in the chickpeas with 3 C. of water.
4. Cook them until they start simmering. Lower the heat and let them cook until the mixture becomes thick for about 1 h.
5. Heat the tortilla in the microwave for few seconds. Transfer it to a serving plate.
6. Spoon the chickpea mixture into the tortilla. Top it with some hot sauce, onion, and cucumber.
7. Fold the tortilla over the filling burrito-style then serve it.
8. Enjoy.

CASHEW Butter Wraps

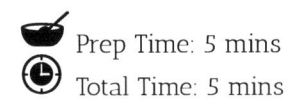

Prep Time: 5 mins
Total Time: 5 mins

Servings per Recipe: 2
Calories	133.5
Fat	0.8g
Cholesterol	0.0mg
Sodium	14.6mg
Carbohydrates	32.4g
Protein	3.3g

Ingredients

8 tbsp raw smooth cashew butter, divided into 2 tsp per leaf
12 romaine lettuce leaves
2 bananas, sliced

Directions

1. Lay 2 tsp of cashew butter in each lettuce leaf.
2. Arrange over it the banana slices then serve them right away.
3. Enjoy.

Spicy Turkey Wraps

Prep Time: 20 mins
Total Time: 40 mins

Servings per Recipe: 8
Calories   80.0
Fat   1.7g
Cholesterol   26.6mg
Sodium   181.4mg
Carbohydrates   4.8g
Protein   10.6g

Ingredients

- 1 medium onion, chopped
- 1 medium sweet potato, peeled and cut into pieces
- 1 (14 oz.) cans low sodium reduced-fat chicken broth
- 3 tbsp diced celery
- 1/2 tsp salt
- 1 tsp sage
- 1/4 tsp black pepper
- 2 C. boneless cooked turkey, cubed
- 3/4 C. seasoned stuffing mix
- 8 (10 inches) whole wheat tortillas
- 2 C. shredded reduced-fat cheddar cheese
- sliced jalapeno pepper

Directions

1. Place a pot over medium heat. Stir in it the onion, sweet potato, chicken broth, celery, salt, sage, and pepper.
2. Cook them until they start simmering. Lower the heat and let them cook for 12 min.
3. Add the stuffing mix with turkey. Let them cook for 6 min while stirring until the mixture becomes thick.
4. Warm a tortilla in the microwave for few seconds. Place it on a serving plate.
5. Spread in the center of it 1/4 C. of cheese followed by 1/2 C. of the turkey mixture.
6. Fold the tortilla over the filling burrito style. Place it in a hot pan and cook it for few seconds on each side.
7. Repeat the process with the remaining cheese, turkey mixture and tortillas.
8. Serve your wraps warm.
9. Enjoy.

WEST AFRICAN
Peanut Wraps

Prep Time: 8 mins
Total Time: 8 mins

Servings per Recipe: 2
Calories   49.6
Fat   2.3g
Cholesterol   0.0mg
Sodium   283.3mg
Carbohydrates   5.9g
Protein   2.4g

Ingredients

- 1 C. cooked shrimp
- 1 tomatoes, seeded and chopped
- 1/4 C. carrot, shredded
- 2 tbsp of mint, chopped
- 1 tsp lemon zest, grated
- 1 tbsp reduced sodium soy sauce
- 1 large fat-free flour tortillas
- 1 tbsp peanuts, chopped

Directions

1. Get a mixing bowl: Toss in it the shrimp, chopped tomato, shredded carrot, chopped mint, grated lemon zest, and soy sauce.
2. Season them with a pinch of salt.
3. Pour the mixture in the center of a tortilla. Fold it burrito style then serve it.
4. Enjoy.

Mexican Tuna Rolls

Prep Time: 5 mins
Total Time: 5 mins

Servings per Recipe: 1
Calories	294.6
Fat	7.5g
Cholesterol	32.3mg
Sodium	500.1mg
Carbohydrates	30.6g
Protein	25.7g

Ingredients

- 1 whole wheat tortilla
- 2 tbsp guacamole
- 0.5 (6 oz.) cans tuna, drained
- 2 medium romaine lettuce leaves
- 1 small tomatoes, sliced

Directions

1. Warm the tortilla in a hot pan for few seconds on each side.
2. Transfer it to a serving plate. Top it with a layer of guacamole, tuna, lettuce, and tomato.
3. Season them with a pinch of salt and pepper. Roll the tortilla over the filling tightly.
4. Slice your tuna roll in half then serve it.
5. Enjoy.

MOSCOW
Beef Wraps

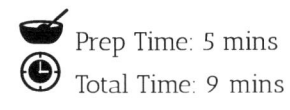

Prep Time: 5 mins
Total Time: 9 mins

Servings per Recipe: 1
Calories   371.9
Fat   22.7g
Cholesterol   111.8mg
Sodium   156.0mg
Carbohydrates   4.0g
Protein   38.0g

Ingredients

1 large whole wheat tortilla
mayonnaise
3 -6 slices roast beef
1/8 C. sliced bell peppers
sliced tomatoes

2 slices swiss cheese
1/8 C. lettuce

Directions

1. Warm the tortilla in the microwave for few seconds.
2. Top it with a layer of a dressing followed by lettuce, tomato, pepper, onion, beef roast, and cheese.
3. Fold the tortilla over the filling burrito-style then serve it.
4. Enjoy.

Chipotle Bean Wraps

Prep Time: 25 mins
Total Time: 25 mins

Servings per Recipe: 4
Calories   399.8
Fat   14.3g
Cholesterol   0.0mg
Sodium   633.1mg
Carbohydrates   56.7g
Protein   13.8g

Ingredients

- 2 tbsp cider vinegar
- 1 tbsp canola oil
- 2 tsp chopped canned chipotle chilies in adobo
- 1/4 tsp salt
- 2 C. shredded red cabbage
- 1 medium carrot, shredded
- 1/4 C. chopped cilantro
- 1 (15 oz.) cans white beans, rinsed
- 1 ripe avocado
- 1/2 C. shredded sharp cheddar cheese
- 2 tbsp minced red onions
- 4 whole wheat tortillas

Directions

1. Get a mixing bowl: Mix in it the vinegar, oil, chipotle chile and salt.
2. Stir in the carrot with cabbage, and cilantro. place it aside.
3. Get a mixing bowl: Mix in it the avocado with beans until they become chunky.
4. Fold the cheese and onion into the mixture.
5. Warm the tortillas in the microwave for few seconds. Top them with a layer of avocado spread followed by cabbage salad.
6. Roll the tortillas over the filling tightly. Serve them immediately.
7. Enjoy.

HOT HAWAIIAN
Wraps

🥣 Prep Time: 10 mins
🕐 Total Time: 40 mins

Servings per Recipe: 6
Calories   558.5
Fat   38.0g
Cholesterol   56.9mg
Sodium   1119.5mg
Carbohydrates   44.0g
Protein   9.5g

Ingredients

1 (20 oz.) cans, pineapple chunks drained
1 lb. turkey bacon
1/2 C. Miracle Whip
1/2 C. chili sauce or sriracha
1 C. brown sugar

Directions

1. Before you do anything, preheat the oven to 400 F.
2. Slice the bacon strips in half.
3. Roll a bacon slice around each pineapple chunk then press into it a toothpick to secure it.
4. Repeat the process with the remaining bacon and pineapple. Lay them in a baking dish.
5. Cook them in the oven for 11 min.
6. Get a mixing bowl: Whisk in it the miracle whip with chili sauce and brown sugar.
7. Drizzle it all over the bacon wraps. Cook them for an extra 22 min in the oven.
8. Serve your chili wraps warm.
9. Enjoy.

Napa Valley Wraps

> Prep Time: 15 mins
> Total Time: 15 mins

Servings per Recipe: 4
Calories   416.7
Fat   9.5g
Cholesterol   0.0mg
Sodium   155.1mg
Carbohydrates   77.8g
Protein   25.0g

Ingredients

3 oranges peeled and sliced.
1/2 avocado
2 sprigs dill
1/2 head napa cabbage, sliced

2 tomatoes, sliced
12 romaine leaves

Directions

1. Get a food processor: Place in it 2 slices oranges with dill and avocado.
2. Blend them smooth to make the dressing.
3. Get a large mixing bowl: Chop the remaining orange and stir it with cabbage and orange dressing.
4. Spoon the mixture into romaine leaves. Garnish them with tomato slices then serve them.
5. Enjoy.

CALIFORNIA WRAPS
with Thai Spicy Mayo

Prep Time: 15 mins
Total Time: 15 mins

Servings per Recipe: 2
Calories 550.4
Fat 30.0g
Cholesterol 60.2mg
Sodium 998.5mg
Carbohydrates 48.9g
Protein 21.5g

Ingredients

Sauce
3 tbsp mayonnaise
1 tbsp Thai sweet chili sauce or garlic sriracha
1 tsp Worcestershire sauce
1 tsp chili powder
1/8 tsp sriracha sauce
Filling
1/2 C. swiss cheese, shredded
1/2 C. cheddar cheese, shredded
1/4 C. spinach, chopped
1/4 C. portabella mushroom, chopped
2 tbsp red bell peppers, chopped
1/4 C. summer squash, grated
3 tbsp sweet onions, chopped
1 tbsp basil, chopped
salt
ground black pepper
2 (10 inches) tortillas
Toppings
chopped tomato
cubed avocado
chips, crushed
mixed sprouts

Directions

1. Get a large mixing bowl: Whisk in it the mayo with sweet chili sauce, Worcestershire sauce, chili powder and Sriracha sauce.
2. Stir in the cheese with spinach, mushrooms, bell pepper, squash, onion, and basil. Sprinkle over them some salt and pepper.
3. Spoon the mixture into the tortillas and fold them. Serve your wraps right away.
4. Enjoy.

Hot Breakfast Wraps

Prep Time: 5 mins
Total Time: 5 mins

Servings per Recipe: 1
Calories	1611.0
Fat	103.6g
Cholesterol	3362.2mg
Sodium	2071.5mg
Carbohydrates	41.0g
Protein	118.4g

Ingredients

- 1 whole wheat tortilla
- 1 tbsp reduced-fat mayonnaise
- 1 tbsp hot sauce
- 2 medium hard-boiled eggs, shelled and chopped
- 4 tbsp sweet onions, chopped
- 6 tbsp lettuce, chopped

Directions

1. Get a mixing bowl: Whisk in it the mayo with hot sauce.
2. Add the eggs with onion, lettuce, a pinch of salt and pepper. Toss them to coat.
3. Spoon the mixture into one side of the tortilla then roll it tightly.
4. Serve your wrap right away.
5. Enjoy.

KETOGENIC
String Bean Wraps

Prep Time: 10 mins
Total Time: 45 mins

Servings per Recipe: 6
Calories 117.2
Fat 7.5g
Cholesterol 10.8mg
Sodium 141.7mg
Carbohydrates 9.9g
Protein 4.4g

Ingredients

2 (15 oz.) cans green beans
12 slices turkey bacon

Directions

1. Before you do anything, preheat the oven to 375 F.
2. Gather 5 green beans in your hands. Wrap around them a bacon slice and place them on a baking sheet.
3. Repeat the process with the remaining ingredients. Season them with a pinch of salt and pepper.
4. Broil them in the oven for 36 min.
5. Enjoy.

Pennsylvania Cheese Wraps

Prep Time: 15 mins
Total Time: 15 mins

Servings per Recipe: 2
Calories   824.6
Fat   55.4g
Cholesterol   108.2mg
Sodium   1502.0mg
Carbohydrates   58.6g
Protein   24.7g

Ingredients

- 1/2 head lettuce, shredded
- 1 carrot, peeled, like potatoes
- Turkey bacon bits, optional
- 1/2 C. diced onion
- 1/4 C. diced garlic
- 1/2 C. softened cream cheese
- 1/4 C. of homemade ranch dressing
- mustard
- meat
- 2 - 3 slices cheese
- 2 wrap sized garlic and herb tortillas

Directions

1. Get a mixing bowl: Combine in it the cream cheese with garlic, ranch dressing, and mustard.
2. Place the tortillas on serving plate. Top them with the cream mixture followed by lettuce, carrot, bacon, and onion.
3. Fold the tortillas over the filling and wrap them in foil.
4. Serve your wraps immediately or place them in the fridge until ready to serve.
5. Enjoy.

ISLAND
Coconut Wraps

Prep Time: 5 mins
Total Time: 10 mins

Servings per Recipe: 1
Calories   316.3
Fat   25.7g
Cholesterol   588.5mg
Sodium   469.4mg
Carbohydrates   1.0g
Protein   18.9g

Ingredients

3 eggs
2 tbsp coconut flour
1 pinch salt

1/4 tsp baking powder
1 tbsp butter

Directions

1. Get a mixing bowl: Mix in it the eggs with flour and salt until they become smooth.
2. Stir in the baking powder.
3. Place a skillet over medium heat. Heat in it 1/2 tbsp of butter. Pour in it half of the batter.
4. Let it cook for 1 to 2 min on each side. Transfer the cake wrap aside and repeat the process with the remaining batter.
5. Serve you cake wraps with your favorite filling.
6. Enjoy.

How to Make Cabbage

Prep Time: 20 mins
Total Time: 40 mins

Servings per Recipe: 6
alories	399.8
Fat	14.3g
Cholesterol	0.0mg
Sodium	633.1mg
Carbohydrates	56.7g
Protein	13.8g

Ingredients

- 1 head cabbage
- 2 tbsp olive oil, or as needed
- 1 small onion, thinly sliced
- 1/2 chopped green bell pepper
- 1 green onion, sliced
- 2 sprigs fresh thyme
- 1 whole Scotch bonnet chile pepper
- 1 tsp salt (optional)
- 1 C. shredded carrots
- 1/4 C. white vinegar
- 2 tbsp white sugar

Directions

1. Discard the outer leaves of the cabbage then discard its head and shred the leaves.
2. Before you do anything else, place a large pan over medium high heat and heat the olive oil in it.
3. Add the onion, green bell pepper, and green onion then cook them for 6 min white stirring them from time to time.
4. Once the time is up, add the thyme, Scotch bonnet pepper, and salt then stir them well.
5. Combine in the shredded carrots and cabbage then put on the lid and let the mix cook for 12 min over low heat while stirring it from time to time.
6. Once the time is up, remove the lid and add the sugar and vinegar to the mix. Let them cook for an extra 4 min.
7. Remove the scotch bonnet pepper along with thyme sprigs then serve your Jamaican cabbage with some bread.
8. Enjoy!

JAMAICAN Cabbage

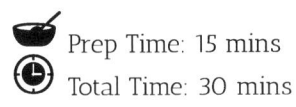

Prep Time: 15 mins
Total Time: 30 mins

Servings per Recipe: 4
Calories   149.0
Fat   7.2g
Cholesterol   0.0mg
Sodium   646.1mg
Carbohydrates   20.6g
Protein   3.8g

Ingredients

1 cabbage, chopped
2 carrots, grated
1/2 C. bell pepper, chopped
1 onion, chopped
1 garlic clove, minced
2 tbsp oil
1/8 tsp allspice

1 tsp salt
1 tsp pepper
1/4 C. water
1/2 scotch bonnet pepper

Directions

1. Place a large skillet over medium heat. Heat the oil in it. Add the onion and cook it for 3 min.
2. Stir in the garlic and cook them for 1 min. Stir in the carrot with cabbage, spices, and water. Put on the lid and cook them for 5 to 7 min until the veggies are cooked.
3. Serve your veggies stir fry with your favorite toppings or with some grilled chicken.
4. Enjoy.

Brown Glazed Carrots

Prep Time: 20 mins
Total Time: 50 mins

Servings per Recipe: 4
Calories   103.8
Fat   3.3g
Cholesterol   7.6mg
Sodium   140.5mg
Carbohydrates   18.6g
Protein   1.3g

Ingredients

- 1 lb carrot, sliced
- 1 tbsp butter
- 2 tbsp brown sugar
- 1 tsp hot sauce
- 1 tsp fresh lemon juice
- 1 tsp orange juice
- 1 tsp ground cumin
- 2 garlic cloves, minced
- 1/4-1/2 tsp chili powder
- salt, to taste

Directions

1. Place a large saucepan over medium heat. Place in it the carrot and pour over it enough water to cover it.
2. Cook them for 12 min until the carrots are soft. Drain it and place it aside.
3. Discard the water from the saucepan. Add the butter to the same saucepan and heat it.
4. Stir in the brown sugar, hot pepper sauce, lemon juice, orange juice (or pineapple juice), cumin, garlic, and chili powder.
5. Cook them for 4 min while stirring all the time to make the sauce. Stir the carrots into the sauce. Serve them warm.
6. Enjoy.

JAMAICAN Roast

Prep Time: 20 mins
Total Time: 1 hr

Servings per Recipe: 6	
Calories	226.1
Fat	11.0g
Cholesterol	108.7mg
Sodium	639.7mg
Carbohydrates	6.3g
Protein	24.7g

Ingredients

3 Cornish hens
1 piece fresh ginger, grated
4 green onions, minced
4 garlic cloves, minced
1 orange, zest of, finely shredded
1/2 orange, juice of
2 limes, juice of
2 limes, zest of
1 tbsp packed brown sugar
1 tbsp soy sauce
1 tsp salt
1 tsp pepper
3/4 tsp ground cinnamon
1/4 tsp ground cloves
3 tbsp canola oil

Directions

1. Get a small mixing bowl: Whisk in it the ginger, onions, garlic, orange zest and juice, lime zest and juice, sugar, soy sauce, salt and pepper, cinnamon, cloves and the oil to make the sauce.
2. Place the marinade aside to sit for 12 min.
3. Before you do anything else, preheat the grill and grease it.
4. Use a sharp knife to slice the hens in half. Place the hens on the grill and cook them for 20 to 25 min on each side over low medium heat while basting them with the sauce.
5. Serve your grilled hen sauces warm.
6. Enjoy.

Nutty Jerk Coleslaw

Prep Time: 10 mins
Total Time: 30 mins

Servings per Recipe: 6
Calories   170.7
Fat   12.9g
Cholesterol   5.0mg
Sodium   151.6mg
Carbohydrates   13.4g
Protein   2.3g

Ingredients

- 4 C. shredded cabbage
- 1/4 C. shredded carrot
- 1/2 C. chopped walnuts
- 1/2 C. mayonnaise
- 2 tbsp sugar
- 1 tbsp cider vinegar
- 1 tbsp Jamaican jerk spice

Directions

1. Get a large mixing bowl: Toss in it the carrots with walnuts, and cabbage.
2. Get a small mixing bowl: Whisk in it the sugar with vinegar, and jerk spice. Drizzle the mix all over the veggies.
3. Place the salad in the fridge until ready to serve.
4. Enjoy.

FLAME BROILED
Sweet Potatoes

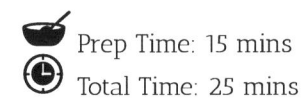

Prep Time: 15 mins
Total Time: 25 mins

Servings per Recipe: 6
Calories   162.9
Fat   3.9g
Cholesterol   10.1mg
Sodium   98.7mg
Carbohydrates   30.7
Protein   1.8g

Ingredients

3 tbsp brown sugar
2 tbsp butter, softened and divided
1 tsp ground ginger
1 tsp dark molasses
1 tsp pineapple juice
1/4 tsp almond extract
1 tbsp cilantro, chopped
1 1/2 lbs sweet potatoes, cleaned, chunked

Directions

1. Before you do anything preheat the grill and grease it.
2. Get a small mixing bowl: Mix in it the brown sugar, ginger, and 1 Tbsp of the butter. Add the molasses, pineapple juice, almond extract and cilantro and mix them well to make the sauce.
3. Place the remaining bowl in a heatproof bowl and microwave it until it melts. Coat the sweet potatoes with the melted butter.
4. Cook the potatoes on the grill for 9 to 12 min or until they become soft.
5. Serve your grilled potatoes with the pineapple sauce.
6. Enjoy.

Simple Banana Chips

Prep Time: 10 mins
Total Time: 30 mins

Servings per Recipe: 25
Calories	45.7
Fat	0.2g
Cholesterol	0.3mg
Sodium	8.0mg
Carbohydrates	10.1g
Protein	1.0g

Ingredients

- 3 bananas
- 1 1/2 C. almond flour
- 1/4 C. almond milk
- 2 -4 tbsp brown sugar
- 1/4 tsp vanilla extract
- 1 pinch salt
- oil

Directions

1. Get a large mixing bowl: Place the bananas in it and mash them until they become smooth.
2. Combine in the sugar, vanilla, milk, salt, and flour. Combine them well until they become smooth.
3. Place a large deep skillet over medium heat. Heat about 1 inch of oil in it. Use a large tbsp of to drop the mix in it.
4. Fry the chips for 2 to 4 min on each side until they become golden brown. Serve them with your favorite sauce.
5. Enjoy.

COCONUT
Cod Stew

🥣 Prep Time: 5 mins
🕐 Total Time: 1 hr 35 mins

Servings per Recipe: 4
Calories 408.2
Fat 23.2g
Cholesterol 73.3mg
Sodium 152.5mg
Carbohydrates 17.7g
Protein 34.5g

Ingredients

- 1 1/2-2 lbs cod fish fillets
- 2 tbsp corn oil
- 3 garlic cloves, minced
- 1 large onion, chopped
- 1 chili, your choice, minced
- 1 tsp black pepper
- 1 1/2-2 C. coconut milk
- 1 C. chopped tomato
- 1 lime, juice of

Directions

1. Season the fish fillets with a some salt. Place them in a roasting pan and refrigerate them for 1 h.
2. Place a large pan over medium heat. Heat the oil it. Sauté in it the garlic, onion, chile and pepper for 6 min while stirring from time to time.
3. Add the tomato with coconut milk. Cook them until they start boiling. Lower the heat and simmer it until half of it evaporates.
4. Once the time is up, run the fish fillets under some cold water to discard the salt. Add it to the pan and let it cook for 12 min.
5. Serve your fish stew with some lime juice.
6. Enjoy.

Skirt Steak Habanero Sauce

Prep Time: 8 mins
Total Time: 18 mins

Servings per Recipe: 8
Calories	193.8
Fat	9.4g
Cholesterol	46.4mg
Sodium	62.5mg
Carbohydrates	1.8g
Protein	24.3g

Ingredients

- 2 lbs flank steaks or top round beef
- 1/2 C. habanero pepper, finely chopped
- 6 tbsp lime juice
- 1/4 C. chopped cilantro
- salt & black pepper

Directions

1. Before you do anything preheat the grill on high heat and grease it.
2. Use a sharp knife to cut the steak into thin slices.
3. Lay plastic sheet on a working surface and lay on it a steak slice. Cover it with a second plastic sheet. Pound it until it becomes 1/4 inch thick.
4. To make the hot sauce: Get a small mixing bowl, mix in it the rest of the ingredients.
5. Coat the steak slices with the 2/3 of the hot sauce. Cook the steak slices on the grill for 3 to 5 min on each side.
6. Serve your steaks warm with the remaining hot sauce.
7. Enjoy.

TROPICAL Prawns Skillet

Prep Time: 10 mins
Total Time: 20 mins

Servings per Recipe: 4
Calories   101.0
Fat   4.1g
Cholesterol   37.8mg
Sodium   251.2mg
Carbohydrates   11.2g3
Protein   5.9g

Ingredients

1 tbsp cooking oil
1 large onion, finely chopped
1 red capsicum, chopped
1 green capsicum, chopped
1/4 tsp dried thyme
1/4 tsp ground allspice
1/4 tsp ground black pepper
1/4 tsp ground cinnamon

1/8 tsp cayenne pepper
1/8 tsp salt
1 (400 g) cans chopped tomatoes
20 large green prawns, or scallops

Directions

1. Place a large skillet over medium heat. Heat the oil in it. Sauté in it the onion and capsicums for 5 min.
2. Add the rest of the ingredients. Let them cook for 4 min or until the prawns are done.
3. Serve your prawns warm with some white rice and enjoy.
4. Enjoy.

Tropical Vegetarian Papaya Soup

Prep Time: 20 mins
Total Time: 55 mins

Servings per Recipe: 4
Calories	221 kcal
Fat	13.8 g
Carbohydrates	16.7g
Protein	11.5 g
Cholesterol	0 mg
Sodium	330 mg

Ingredients

- 2 tbsp coconut oil
- 1 small onion, chopped
- 3/4 C. red bell pepper, chopped
- 6 fresh chives, chopped
- 3 cloves garlic, minced
- 1 tbsp chopped fresh rosemary
- 3 fresh sage leaves, chopped
- 2 tsp thinly sliced fresh ginger
- 1 small hot chili pepper (optional)
- 1 (14 oz.) package firm tofu, drained and cut into 3/4-inch cubes
- salt to taste
- 2 tbsp vegetarian Worcestershire sauce
- 1/2 tsp lime juice
- 6 C. water
- 3 cubes vegetable bouillon
- 1 small green papaya, peeled and cut into chunks
- 1 bunch fresh spinach, trimmed
- 1 tbsp fried onions

Directions

1. In a soup pan, melt the coconut oil on medium heat and sauté the onion, red bell pepper, chives, garlic, rosemary, sage, ginger and chili pepper for about 1 minute. Add the tofu and cook for about 6 minutes, stirring after every 2 minutes. Stir in the salt, Worcestershire sauce and lime juice.
2. In a bowl, add the water and bouillon and mix till dissolved.
3. Place the bouillon mixture over the tofu mixture and bring to a simmer.
4. Add the papaya and simmer, covered loosely for about 20 minutes.
5. Remove from the heat and immediately, stir in the spinach.
6. Keep aside, covered for about 2-3 minutes.
7. Serve the soup hot with a topping of the fried onions.

SPICY MANGO
Papaya Salsa

Prep Time: 20 mins
Total Time: 20 mins

Servings per Recipe: 4
Calories	35 kcal
Fat	0.2 g
Carbohydrates	9 g
Protein	0.7 g
Cholesterol	0 mg
Sodium	2 mg

Ingredients

1/2 small ripe mango, peeled and cubed
1/2 small papaya, peeled, seeded and cubed
1/2 small onion, diced
1 clove garlic, minced
1 fresh jalapeno pepper, seeded and diced
1/4 red bell pepper, diced
1/4 orange bell pepper, diced
1 lime, juiced
salt and freshly ground black pepper to taste

Directions

1. In a large bowl, mix together the mango, papaya, onion, garlic, jalapeño pepper, bell peppers, lime juice, salt and pepper.
2. Serve immediately.

Papaya Boats

Prep Time: 15 mins
Total Time: 15 mins

Servings per Recipe: 4
Calories   190 kcal
Fat   5.3 g
Carbohydrates   33.4g
Protein   5.7 g
Cholesterol   1 mg
Sodium   52 mg

Ingredients

- 1 C. fat-free plain yogurt
- 1/4 C. walnuts
- 1/4 C. raisins
- 1 C. chopped fresh strawberries
- 2 medium papayas, cut in half lengthwise and seeded
- 2 tbsp honey

Directions

1. In a bowl, mix together the yogurt, walnuts and raisins.
2. Gently, fold in the strawberries.
3. Divide the mixture into the centers of the papaya halves evenly.
4. Serve with a drizzling of the honey.

AVOCADO
Papaya Salsa

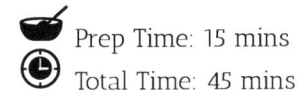

Prep Time: 15 mins
Total Time: 45 mins

Servings per Recipe: 8
Calories	77 kcal
Fat	3.9 g
Carbohydrates	11g
Protein	1.1 g
Cholesterol	0 mg
Sodium	5 mg

Ingredients

1 mango - peeled, seeded and diced
1 papaya - peeled, seeded and diced
1 large red bell pepper, seeded and diced
1 avocado - peeled, pitted and diced
1/2 sweet onion, peeled and diced

2 tbsp chopped fresh cilantro
2 tbsp balsamic vinegar
salt and pepper to taste

Directions

1. In a bowl, mix together the mango, papaya, red bell pepper, avocado, sweet onion, cilantro, balsamic vinegar, salt and pepper.
2. Refrigerate, covered to chill for at least 30 minutes before serving.

Island Juice

Prep Time: 10 mins
Total Time: 10 mins

Servings per Recipe: 8
Calories   61 kcal
Fat   0.1 g
Carbohydrates   15.4 g
Protein   0.5 g
Cholesterol   0 mg
Sodium   5 mg

Ingredients

- 1 C. sliced mango
- 1 C. diced, peeled papaya
- 1 C. orange juice
- 1/4 C. lime juice
- 1/4 C. white sugar
- 1 tsp grated orange zest
- 4 C. water

Directions

1. In a blender, place the mango and papaya and pulse till smooth.
2. Add the orange juice, lime juice, sugar, orange zest and water and pulse till well combined.
3. Serve over the crushed ice.

ENJOY THE RECIPES?

KEEP ON COOKING WITH 6 MORE FREE COOKBOOKS!

Visit our website and simply enter your email address to join the club and receive your 6 cookbooks.

http://booksumo.com/magnet

https://www.instagram.com/booksumopress/

https://www.facebook.com/booksumo/

Printed in Great Britain
by Amazon